No More Time

No More Time

GREG DELANTY

LOUISIANA STATE UNIVERSITY PRESS
BATON ROUGE

Published by Louisiana State University Press
www.lsupress.org

LSU Press Paperback Original

DESIGNER: Michelle A. Neustrom
TYPEFACES: Sabon and Optima

COVER IMAGE: Drawing of aye-aye by Amber Geneva

LIBRARY OF CONGRESS CATALOGING-IN-PUBLICATION DATA

Names: Delanty, Greg, 1958– author.
Title: No more time / Greg Delanty.
Description: Baton Rouge : Louisiana State University Press, [2020]
Identifiers: LCCN 2020002996 (print) I LCCN 2020002997
    (ebook) I ISBN 978-0-8071-7235-3 (paperback : acid-free paper) I
    ISBN 978-0-8071-7426-5 (pdf) I ISBN 978-0-8071-7427-2 (epub)
Subjects: LCGFT: Poetry.
Classification: LCC PR6054.E397 N6 2020 (print) I LCC PR6054.
    E397 (ebook) I DDC 821/.914--dc23
LC record available at https://lccn.loc.gov/2020002996
LC ebook record available at https://lccn.loc.gov/2020002997

This book is for everyone, of course,
but it is especially dedicated to all those who
work to slow climate change. The book is also
especially dedicated to my son, Dan Delanty;
my nieces, Niamh Delanty and Saorlaith Delanty;
and Greta Thunberg, Phinn Clason, Spencer Clason,
Yvie MacDonald Dowd and all future generations.
We want you to know, and not just for ourselves,
that some of the people gone before you
are trying not to let you down.

CONTENTS

PART 3. A Field Guide to People (continued)

PREFATORY NOTE

Extinction is a natural phenomenon. It occurs at a natural "background" rate of about one to five species per year. Scientists estimate we are now losing species at one thousand to ten thousand times the background rate. Dozens go extinct every day. There have been other mass extinctions in the past, but as the American Museum of Natural History has engraved on its floor, the current rate is caused "solely by humanity's transformation of the ecological landscape."

The distinction between humans and other animals is unclear, just as the distinction between poetry and other writing is unclear. Consider what follows as writing by an animal.

No More Time

Proem

LOOSESTRIFE

You have become your name, loosestrife,
        carried on sheep, spurting up out of ballast,
a cure brought across the deep
        to treat wounds, soothe trouble.
There have been others like you, the rhododendron,
        the cattails that you in your turn overrun.
Voices praise your magenta spread, your ability
        to propagate by seed, by stem, by root,
and how you adjust to light, to soil, spreading
        your glory across the earth even as you kill
by boat, by air, by land all before you: the hardy iris,
        the rare orchids, the spawning ground of fish.
You'll overtake the earth and destroy even yourself.
        Ah, our loosestrife, purple plague, beautiful us.

PART 1

A Field Guide to People

Aye-Aye

The name of this lemur, which has an unusually long middle finger,
is derived from a person's alarmed utterance on seeing the animal.

So that's how the name came about, aye-aye.
Solitary shade, spirit of the night,
your face caught in the light seems to ask why

you're given no quarter, shot on sight.
The picture shows your bat-eared head,
large as a baby's, staring in fright.

Your extraterrestrial, wide-eyed dread
and manicured long nails scare,
magnify into nightmare. Folks are misled

by their imaginations to needless fear.
You are the bringer of bad luck, harbinger
of death. Aye-aye, you continue to glare

back, your face a mirror, terror's dead ringer.
With a long middle digit you give the finger.

Bos taurus

*The raising of cattle adds to climate change, partly due to the methane
produced by bacteria in the stomachs of cows.*

They're such a part of our life, *Bos taurus.*
We take for granted the silk of milk for tea,
bullions of butter, the panoply of cheese, plus:

they haul loads, pull plows, act as money,
a dowry, are a daily staple, and so much more.
You browse a meat aisle: filet mignon, sirloin, kidney?

What's tender? There's a deal on veal? Forget the poor
calf. Scruples flit like flies around the tail of a cow.
Quell your qualms, man. You're a natural carnivore.

Whatever you do, don't look at your hooves now.
You're standing in their skins. Such a bleeding heart.
Your default: headless hen, bleatless lamb, ass of sow.

And gas, you ruefully laugh, loading milk in the cart,
thinking of what the billions of cattle burp and fart.

Chimpanzee

As a chimp, usually the adult male,
approaches and the roar of the water
booms louder, you see him, without fail,

hurry up. His demeanor starts to alter,
hair bristling. Arriving at the fall,
he stands, sways from one foot to the other,

bows, genuflects. Answering some call,
he dips his hand as if in holy water, plashes
head and shoulders in the flowing prayer shawl,

tests the ropes of draping vines, lashes
his body securely to several, takes flight
over the deafening water as it crashes.

He swings like a thurible above that veil of white;
the spray is the incense of the monkey's water rite.

Dusky Seaside Sparrow

Merritt Island, Florida, was flooded in order to eradicate mosquitoes around the Kennedy Space Center, destroying this sparrow's only nesting ground.

Beautiful, the dusky seaside sparrow.
That's all the bird is now, a classy name.
Here today, gone before tomorrow.

The star-speckled birds haven't much claim.
Surely, they should have had the foresight
to spread farther afield, not rely on the same

ten square miles, taken flight
if only a short way beyond Merritt Island,
nested in the tall saw grass out of sight.

They should have known of the work in hand,
the zillion-dollar exploration of deep space.
Their space was nothing to something so grand.

Maddening mosquitoes are murderous to erase.
The sparrows are collateral damage in this case.

Elephant

Sometimes you see something so dire, so
dreadful that the mind's camera
instantly shoots a video of the scenario,

a close-up, lasers it into your retina,
a replayed flashback for as long as you live:
a teacher thrashing a child, or the trauma

of an elephant we saw given a sedative
so she could rest that time in Dublin Zoo.
The aged female was trapped in a repetitive

back and forth on her haunches, unable to
stop herself. Her keeper explained to us
that for years she had been confined, locked into

a circus van. Her only way to move in this Orcus
was to rock. "Rescuing her was our unforgettable bonus."

Falls-of-the-Ohio Scurfpea

I feel like a student in my Environment 101,
crushed by daily news: creatures going or gone,
the changing climate, the planet under the gun.

In teacher mode I tell them: "For yourselves press on,
your own well-being. You're entitled to be happy.
Action makes life fun. Good news: the café marron

and sage grouse are saved." I say nothing of the scurfpea,
Orbexilum stipulatum. Its modest flower
blending with white-bearded cascades. A century

or more and not a single sighting along the river
at Rock Island. It relied too much on the bison.
You know how one thing depends on another,

with the jowled ones diminished, so went this 'un;
finally condemned with the building of US Dam 21.

Golden Toad

It has been established that global climate change
is directly linked to the extinction of species. The
golden toad is an example.
    — J. Alan Pounds

When did you last see a toad or frog
on the side of the road, in your garden,
hopping across a wood or skirting a bog?

They were everywhere back when
we were tadpoles. Remember being told
that if you as much as brushed one,

you'd wake covered in warts. You loved to hold
them pulsing in your palm, each a Buddha,
proptosed-eyed, and slimy cold.

It seems people have upset the dharma
of toads and frogs, including this gold glory.
We play carelessly with our mother's karma,

irking the climate gods and their siblings. Scary
to read frogs and toads are our coal miners' canary.

Honeybee

It is time. Anoint thy tongue with honey,
local thyme honey from Spili, a gift
from the Greek poet Kalogeris, amusedly

musing: "Honey to give your words wing-lift.
Back in the day, it was taken by the Delphic bee."
Wake up, get busy, make a move, a shift,

apply propolis pronto. Impossible not to be
a drama queen nowadays. Without *Apis*
the abyss will take over, unbloom many

a garden, field and wood. The honeybees
are more waning than waxing, warns apiology:
queens, drones, nurses, guards, whole communities.

Protect them, the amber labor force of ecology.
Already, this word-comb is a fossilized apology.

Ibex

In January 2000, the Pyrenean ibex (Spanish common name "bucardo") became extinct. Scientists cloned DNA from a last female.

In the end, no cliff or impossible crag
could save them from plantation or gun.
Their heads hang on walls. Hunters brag.

Many were taken down for sheer fun.
The king pucks—their antler plumes
rising magisterially—plugged one by none.

Gone the clash of horn scimitars, grooms
battling to mate, the *bucardo* of lore.
White-coated gods in lab rooms

summoned one from the dark shore
of the underworld. They should have known
from the ancient myths what was in store.

She returned after seven minutes, lone clone,
relieved to be back among the herds of her own.

The Jellyfish Tree

Medusagyne survives on Mayé Island.
Hanging by her fingertips to a granite cliff,
remnant and revenant of Gondwanaland.

She is a natural hieroglyph
of a time before our time, a beauty
before our beauty. It is as if

she's betting her turn will come again, a tree
better suited to aridity, not the sweaty air
of this archipelago, such temerity.

She is called after a goddess of fear,
Gorgonian, guardian, protectress,
apotropaic, Medusa herself. Best not stare

at her head hanging from the hand of Perseus,
out of which sprang the pinioned horse, Pegasus.

Kāmaʻo

Imagine a place, a zone, an underworld
which includes more than our own kind:
the green and moving ones: ferns with curled

violin necks, gloaming players who grind
their wings together. And listen, the music,
the strain of this bird lingers in the wind.

What flute-like notes, what warbling, what a lick
of trills and whistles. Can you hear its song?
Heard melodies are sometimes sweeter. A trick

of the breeze, zephyr? Things went wrong
with land clearing. Hurricane season
intensified, uprooted trees, and before long

mosquitoes multiplied in rainstorm stagnation.
The song: a figment of my birdbrained imagination.

The Lion

has the humorless, bearded face of an Amish elder
as he patrols the edge of the pride. The females
nurse the cubs with a strictness that is tender.

The young gambol, snap at each other's tails,
prelapsarian, oblivious of threats,
typical of youngsters. He catalogues details,

sniffs the humid atmosphere, frets.
Something alerts him—a hunter or rogue lion
in the tall savanna grass? Whatever upsets

the pride is unknown, but, like a wagon train,
they form a circle, as if with one will,
the same that earlier brought down, *coup de main,*

an elephant with the natural savagery of the kill.
The savanna draws taut, finger-on-the-trigger still.

Monarch Butterfly

A monarch has landed on the rainbow deck chair,
presumably taking a breather from her odyssey
of thousands of miles. Dear soul, rest there,

soak up the sun. We know that your journey
has its own cyclops, sirens, Scylla, that you
will need Aeolus's assistance. Silly

to think myth maps apply solely to us human crew.
The blueprint of the House of Atreus
is imprinted in our molecules. We seem to

ignore the house is coming down around us,
that nature will enforce its own inhuman laws.
The heated gods rally on Mount Olympus.

You fold the V of your wings, hold them in a pause,
in prayer, then open and close them in applause.

PART 2

Breaking News

For ages we took little notice, put any
troublesome thought out of our heads,
knocked on wood, joked she was simply

aging, no need to worry, that the threads
of her memory were unraveling naturally.
But eventually our unanswered dreads

nudge us reluctantly into belated reality.
Daily she finds herself lost, asking where
she is and who, in heaven's name, is she?

Our slow realization redoubles despair.
She doesn't even recognize us. What hell
she gives everyone, even those who care.

Her aging body is becoming a living shell,
Terra Mater, the erasing of cell after cell.

Apathy Is Out

There's not a fly, moth, bee,
woman or man
whose welfare's not our responsibility;
to ignore their predicament
isn't on.
There's not a person in Mad Valley
we shouldn't sit with
and keep company, since
they're sick in the head
on our behalf.

There's not a place, stream or bush,
however remote; or a flagstone
north, south, east or west
that we shouldn't consider
with affection and sympathy.
No matter how far South Africa,
no matter how distant the moon,
they're part of us by right:
there's not a single spot anywhere
we're not a part of. We issue from everywhere.

Translated from Seán Ó Ríordáin

Counting

You try to snap out of it, not think, think
otherwise, say you matter in whatever small
way possible along with the nearly 8 billion other
you-mans inhabiting our terrestrial ball. A figure
it would take 250 years, give or take, to count to
if each number is given a second, but by then
your second would be long up. Blink, a second,
blink you're born, blink gone; no, blink you are
born and gone. What can you do, an unbeliever,
unable to fall back on the Grand Eternal Unblink
and his assurance *you matter more to Him than
a flock of birds,* which to most believing blinks
means you're not worth much? You yourself
would consider that a high compliment being such
a bird lover, especially of the goldfinch nesting
in your garden, weathering Vermont winters.
The males each spring turn bright yellow, the color
of happiness. Seeing them at the sunflower feeder
gives you a lift. They appear fixed entirely on
their own lives, concentrated, vital. Hovering,
they remind you of the hummingbirds supping
from your ruby feeder, the feeder resembling
the votive mantle on the candelabra in St. Mary's.
You'd slip the penny through the slot, light
a candle in the fluttering red glass, pray
a child's prayer for all the poor and suffering
of the world.
            Today watching hummingbirds,
the penny dropped again, pleasurably clinking,
bringing you to your senses, thinking how fast

the hummingbird beats its wings at the votive,
50 times a second and not just up-and-down,
but each time rotating their wings in a figure 8,
which means there's no start or end to each beat,
storing sweetness in their ruby throats.
Tell them they don't count. Tell them
they're nothing.
                    Now, tell yourself.

While Reading the Diary of
Christopher Columbus

The weather's like April in Andalucía, with zephyrs,
  and the morning's a delight—shades
of that day merging with today. Everything's
  becoming everything.
A shimmering, red-bodied damselfly alights
  on our deck.
Takes off again. She zips open space,
  winging it back
and forth from place and time, now
  on my diary,
then back to Don Cristóbal Colón on this Friday
  the thirteenth, lucky as any day,
to inform him he might have stayed at home,
  that the trove is here
andhereandhere, the mirabilia of the Now World.
  And look, the bluebottle,
who yesterday was wingèd disease, has turned
  into a gem glimmering on today's flyleaf,
straight off the Queen of Now's diadem.

The Great Ship

Even non-believers sang for the solace of song.
   —from a record of one of the survivors of the *Titanic*

Later tonight it's to turn cold, the old, sudden,
sharp iceberg cold of New England.

Crickets, cicadas, grasshoppers and frogs play on.
What their song, their wing-music, is saying

we can't say, except they must know already
that the ice has gashed a gaping hole in the hull

of Indian summer, and they are the quartet
that comes out on deck and plays away

as the great ship goes down. We listen quietly
from our deck's lifeboat. *Nearer, my God, to thee.*

Nearer to thee. Play on, brave, noble souls. Play on.

Pumping Gas

Pull the one-armed bandit,
watch the figures race
well above 350.

High Coup

        A jet
        trails
        a line
of coke a c   r   o   s   s the sky's blue
        marble
        counter-
        top

The Red Eye

A middle-aged woman weeps down the aisle,
rests her head against the windowpane.
Her dyed loam-brown hair is out of style,

gray creeps back at the roots. I rack my brain.
She reminds me of someone I can't put a finger on.
Who knows why in the world she cries, what pain

or hurt? I want to ask her if I can
help, if she's okay. Perhaps she'd not be
embarrassed, welcome concern.

While I shilly-shally, she
closes her eyes, nowhere else now to go
but sleep. The angle of her head on the pane reminds me

of the tilt of the earth. Bingo,
I knew she looked familiar: Gaia, leaning on the window.

The Good Old Days

Well, I suppose, we can think of it this way:
inclement weather forecast, "dropping below
zero around dawn, a windchill factor by midday

of minus 60, high winds reaching no
less than 80 miles per hour, a possibility
of freezing rain by nightfall." And our roof

has gaping holes; there's hardly
a window left to break, the burglarproof
door's wide open. We really

do not have a care in the world,
except the to-do list: fix the front doorbell,
polish the windows, get your hair cut or curled,

pick up the dry-cleaning, mow the grass,
collect the kids, but first a pit stop for gas.

Umbilical

You bike most everywhere these days,
wary of your part in the latest war, the slaughter
of innocents, the various wily ways

we've grown used to, complicity's tether.
The gas pump is an umbilical cord
sucking the life out of *Terra Mater.*

You read about leaders ready to award
the future her body, smother
her in her own fumes. You know the reward,

the fate of those who kill their mothers.
Remember *Orestes* you translated to *Humankind.*
Down swoop the Erinyes, the avenging daughters,

driving tormented Orestes out of his mind.
No escaping the Furies now, the ever so kind.

Breaking News

It is below zero outside and we set fire
to our house in the middle of nowhere
to warm ourselves. Our very own pyre.
Look, here comes the fire brigade, flying
the flag. Pumped uniforms pour out, uncoil
black snakes. They assure us everything
is OK as they hose our home with jets of oil.

On viewing *The Roses of Heliogabalus*

Emperor Heliogabalus and his cronies sought to confound the order
of seasons and climates, to sport with the passions and prejudices of
his subjects, and subvert every law of nature and decency.
   —Edward Gibbon, *The History of the Decline and Fall of the
   Roman Empire*

The emperor and his hobnobbing retinue
        recline on the high dais. Everyone gazes
                up at them from the floor. He winks to his chosen few,
                        mutters, "Watch this for a trap," hollers, "Let's
                                play. Bring on the grand finale,"

drinks his cup—a sign to drop the false ceiling of flowers
        on everybody below. You can feel
                nauseating petals catch in noses
                        and crying throats,
                                levels rapidly rising,
                                        drowning everyone in pink roses.

S

With the snaky handle of just one letter, the word,
unsheathed from its scabbard, becomes sword.

A Sentence

Christ,

it wasn't Pilate sentenced the good shepherd to die,

but
the
un-
ruly
cit
i
zens,
the
likes
of
you
and
me.

State of the Union

"Dear Fellow Citizens,
the answer to all our problems is around the bend.
We have struggled tirelessly to arrive at this end:
    the problem of fuel: solved
    the problem of poverty: solved
    the problem of skin color: solved
    the mistreatment of women: solved
    the mistreatment of children: solved
    the mistreatment of forests: solved
    the mistreatment of creatures: solved
    the destruction of our waters: solved
    gun violence: solved
    health care: solved
    endless wars: solved
    drug cartels: solved
    human trafficking: solved
    in short: you name it: solved.

This legacy we'll bequeath our kids' kids' offspring
(maybe even our own kids). They'll thank us. Keep doing
what you do: drive your cars, burn coal, eat beef, invest.
Leave the world to us at our behest.
No need for any distress.
Thank you, and God bless."

Spiritus Mundi

What's the substance called, concealed in fast food,
snacks, soda, a kind of consumer tapeworm,
that makes us crave more, never satisfied?

The stuff of myth, akin to Erysichthon, earth-
tearer, who, having axed trees, is possessed by Famine,
consumes everything till all that's left is his own flesh;

the Hungry Ghosts, their giraffe necks so narrow
they can never stuff enough down at any one time
to fill their humongous stomachs;

or that psychedelic vision of the demon of Gluttony
lodged in the King of Cork, eating all
his subjects out of house and home.

These lesser-known demons can't wait in the wings
any longer. They jostle each other, hungry
to take center stage. They have come into their own.

From *The Vision of Mac Conglinne*

. . . It is a meaningful vision I had last night. If you give me
a break I'll go on. Manchin, the king of Cork's right-hand
man, said, "No way," but the incorrigible poet recited his
vision anyway:

What a mind-blowing, mouthwatering trip,
what a feast for the eyes, what a vision
I had, let me tell you.
A boat of solid suet
was moored in a creamy cove
above the world's calm ocean.

We boarded that cog, charged out
to sea on the choppy surface,
pulling hard on the oars
across the milky plains,
leaving a wake of seaweed,
a spume of honey-colored sand.

On the other side of the water
we reached a fabulous fort
with ramparts of thick custard,
a drawbridge made of fresh butter,
the embankment of harvest wheat,
the palisades of juicy rashers.

The whole structure was spot-on,
rising mighty there.
I entered under
the stringy drapes of dry meat,
over a threshold of croutons.
Its wall was made of cottage cheese.

The pillars of moldy blue
were set in boiled crubeens
—trotters trotting one after the other.
Joists of thick curd,
rafters of frozen yogurt
supported the whole show.

There was a well of wine at the back,
a stream of mead and mulled ale.
No tastier watering hole.
There were hops for brewing stout.
On top was a spring of malt
brimming from the floor.

A pool of colcannon
under a thick batter
lay between that and the ocean.
It was bordered by wedges of butter
glazed with lard
on the outer wall.

Rows of aromatic apple trees,
a rosy orchard in full bloom,
flourished between it and the hill.
A garden of veggies—leeks,
cabbages, carrots and onions—
grew at the back as well.

It was a warm, bright household
full of foxy, well-fed men
lounging around.
Seven torcs and collars

of cheese, tripe and drisheen
adorned each man's neck.

The lord of the manor,
dressed in a corn-beef cloak,
stood next to his elegant wife.
The head chef was there also
at the sizzling spit,
a mighty fork strapped to his back.

The good king would appreciate
a bard reciting at the dinner table,
an enjoyable performance,
a real treat
to hear that lay of the boat
voyaging Milky Way.

Manchin wised up as it dawned on him that the reciting of
such a corker, psychedelic vision would coax the insatiable
demon from King Cork's swollen belly and save their world.

Trees

stand in silence
the way citizens stand
outside a church, city hall or party office
in a speechless vigil
saying, "Listen, wake up.
You are our sisters and brothers.
Without us you're nothing; without us
you will be nothing.
Save us. We are the ventriloquists of silence."

One More Time,

call the earth female, as of old.
She needs to be placed pronto
in the recovery position, gently hold

her chin up, bend the left arm at the elbow,
hand above the head, palm facing down
—waving goodbye or hello?

Set the right arm straight and in line
with her side. Quickly tuck the left foot
up against the right knee. Watch for a sign

of breathing. Don't forget to clear out
the mouth, airways. She may need the kiss
of life. She'll recover for sure, only without

us maybe. Who then will tell her we miss
her? Who then will tell her how dear she is?

Quiz Time

Surely, you will get, know, guess, who
this one is? They go with the current,
never against, in contrast to

the nektons. As varied and different
as an ox from a bee, lizard from kangaroo.
To say they are diverse is understatement.

We know them not so much by who
they are but by where they float and sway.
Perhaps one touched you out of the blue

while you were in for a swim. What an array.
We can't manage without them. They detox
the air. If only we learned to live the same way,

flout extinction's law, all live together in flux:
google "Gause's Law" and "the Plankton Paradox."

24-Rayed Sunstar

If a ray of this starfish is broken off, it can grow back into a new sunstar.

For *Heliaster solaris* things sure look dim.
No sightings for years, a victim of El Niño.
No Houdini act, no shedding of a limb

is enough to escape warming waters, and no
turning the tide. Mourn for this mini sun,
this mini star, banded mystery, whose glow

reaches us long after it's done.
But maybe there's still hope. Maybe.
Should you come across one,

tear the star's self-repairing mystery
ray by ray by ray. Let it populate,
until it begets a starry new galaxy.

Don't we do the same ourselves daily, re-create
newer selves out of injury, despair, even hate?

Earthworm

They face in opposite directions to reproduce.

What a miner, pistoning in slow
motion through the underworld of the earth,
engineering vents, channels, water flow,

converting death and dearth,
day in, night out. Each eyeless body
digesting the soil, nursing birth.

Cut in two, they double, breathe via marly
skin, a must for farm and garden: alfalfa,
spuds, spinach, carrots, cabbage, barley,

wasabi, wheat, gourds, rutabaga, papaya,
endive. You name it. Build them a shrine.
May these lowly laborers of Gaia

multiply, flourish, never decline,
stick with worm love, position 69.

Canticle of the Sun

A secular take, with apologies to Francis of Assisi

Chalk it down. Never so much as now should we praise
    the maker. First, let us praise Brother Sun. He
is the light that alights out of every night. He is
    the radiant first offspring of the One.
Next let us praise Sister Moon, and all the stars like manna
    showering down from the heavens.
Let us praise Weather himself: the twins Air and Wind,
    Cloud and Sky who sustain all creatures.
What about their sibling, Water? She is so humble
    she's hardly noticed. We'd be nothing without her.
Likewise our friend Fire. And laud Mother Earth.
    carrying her basket overflowing
with sundry victuals to feed all her offspring:
    the ant, cow, rat, bee, vulture, bird
of paradise, crow, whale, camel, rainbow trout; all
    our close relatives. Applaud also folks who work
for her sake, especially now we need them more
    than ever. They know we have
so little time, that we've made our mother ill.
    Praise those who say there is hope still, and those
who struggle for peace peacefully. They'll be crowned
    in the maker's goodness before the end,
which is always now and without end. We could go on,
    but let us finish by praising Father Death, for he is
of the creator. Those who do not honor him bring him on us
    before our time. Yet those who struggle for our mother
know another life. May they thrive. Yea, I say, chalk it down.

Any Way You Look at It

No more time no more time no more time no
more time no more time no more time no more
time no more time no more time no more time
no more time no more time no more time no
more time no more time no more time no more
time no more time no more time no more time
no more time no more time no more time no
more time no more time no more time no more
time no more time no more time no more time
no more time no more time no more time no
more time no more time no more time no more
time no more time no more time no more time
no more time no more time no more time no
more time no more time no more time no more

On a Friend Visiting
the Vietnam War Memorial

That mirroring wall: the litany
of names on shiny black stone.
You say we all should go, "Uncanny

to see yourself there, your own
reflection amidst them all,
the untimely dead we can't disown."

I say nothing, imagine such a wall
listing plants and creatures since Noah
that we've undone, a roll call:

paradise parrot, Cape lion, great auk, moa,
Guam flying fox, dusky seaside sparrow,
St. Helena olive, passenger pigeon, quagga,

laughing owl, Cry violet, Steller's sea cow,
Caspian tiger, and more and more now&now

PART 3

A Field Guide to People
(continued)

Northern Gastric Frog

The creature's extinction is attributable to the human introduction
of pathogenic fungi into their native range.

This one was a bit of an artist, especially
the female, so oddly fecund.
At home in backwater rocky

cascades and riffles. Hard to find,
to spot even when plentiful,
its stone-hued skin and sepia behind

blending in. After the female
laid eggs, in vitro fertilized by her groom,
she swallowed them whole,

turned her stomach into a burgeoning womb.
Six weeks later she gave birth within
and out of her own mouth. No more room

for lungs, she breathed through her own skin,
spewed up her mites, each wearing a clown-sad grin.

Oryza sativa

Something to behold, how this crop succeeds
in such diverse moraine. Best of all, see row
after row descend gradually from the gods

down mountainsides to the valleys below,
tiers of a great amphitheater,
their heads craning to watch the show:

the traffic, rickshaws, the helter-skelter
of our priceless world. On the slow train
to Kandy, I was a passing spectator,

watched locals kneeling to the god of rain,
lay offerings to the assisting oxen and ant,
petition the god of rice for healthy grain.

I wanted to join them, genuflect, pray, chant
praise to the plant that's half the world's constant.

Photoautotrophs

Have you ever been given the kiss of life? You
have, you know. You're getting it right now,
every five seconds or so, depending what you do:

running for the bus, swimming, reading. Feel how
the green leaves press on your mouth and nose.
Your chest falls and rises. They silently bow

on their knees above you. You're lost in the daily throes,
unconscious as the girl (at the time) I resuscitated
back to life in my beach-guard days. She insists she owes

me the rest of her years, emailed again lately, reiterated
thanks, updated news of her kids, "who'd be nowhere
without you—they're a breath of fresh air." She restated

wanting to stand me a beer. I raise my downed pint here,
propose a toast to the glass brimming with nothing but air.

Quagga

This chimeric beast, part zebra, part donkey,
—its name the phantom sound
of its supposed call—enjoyed the society

of ostrich and gnu, foraged remote grassland.
So comically mythical: the striped head
a kind of convict's shirt, each band

fading until midbody it bled
into a rufous rear, and on to a white tail
(the last sad male to be found was bred

with a flummoxed horse, producing a female
striped in reverse, from waist to rear).
It's as if a circus clown ran out of a final pail

of white paint. The only photoed quagga, a mare,
stares back from behind bars with an accusing glare.

Rafflesia arnoldii

The corpse flower, a flower straight out of hell
on earth, not one to give your wife or grandmothers
come Valentine's Day, or wear on your lapel.

Though the sight of this particular flower's
measled, fleshy-skinned, monstrous petal
wouldn't help you any, what overpowers

is the stench of rotting flesh and organs: *Chanel
de Cadaver, Bouquet Putrid, Carrion Mystique,
Essence de Carcass, Versense Pong, Allure Hell,*

luring every bug in the vicinity to the reek,
unable to resist entering the rank volcano
of this hottie, and presto, another sprouts in a week.

Meanwhile, the forests of Sumatra and Borneo
are being cleared. Ergo the corpse flower also.

St. Helena Olive

Far-fetched that plants feel pain,
but there's evidence, the experts say,
they can learn, process and retain;

that they've intelligence in some way.
This one's had it: St. Helena olive.
As soon as people settled to stay,

spread, the plant gave up the will to survive.
Natural. And natural also that planters cut
all before them, needing somewhere to live,

to settle themselves. Too late
by the time anybody got it together,
grappled to keep the native alive, bust a gut.

The seeds of this tree refused to flower,
their act of civil disobedience, flower power.

Tarantula Hawk Wasp

Give us a break, man, you with your inventory
of whales crooning to one another,
the society of bees, the scratched history

of bears, elephants mourning a dead mother,
the varying duet of the babakoto,
the St. Helena olive's flower power.

You elect them denizens of a kind of *Paradiso*.
But consider the likes of a particular wasp,
the tarantula hawk, straight out of *The Inferno*.

This one would make Hannibal Lecter gasp.
The wasp's sting turns the tarantula into a zombie,
drugs and drags the spider off in its relentless grasp,

lays an egg in the spider's belly; the larva methodically
eats the host alive; more nature's norm than anomaly.

Umbrella Bird

You never saw anything like this bird,
black from coif to claw, with looks to kill
(though ungainly in flight). But, what's absurd

isn't so much the unusual hairstyle,
which is less like a man's umbrella
than an Elvis quiff, driving many a girl

out of her tree, screeching for her fella,
nor is it his Elvis song, the testosterone bass
crooning longingly for his Priscilla.

But the instrument, and not just that, but the place
it arises from, his throat, a back-to-front tail,
that opens into a feather duster when he plays

his well-endowed come-on, larger in the male,
a kind of didgeridoo, moaning, enticing the female.

The *Voilà* Grouse

I'm pleased that we collectively continue to make great
progress on addressing threats to this bird, conserving
the sagebrush habitat and providing a path forward for
sustainable economic development.
  —US Secretary of the Interior, Sally Jewell,
    September 21, 2016

You should see their fancy costumes:
white ruffs, spectacular fanned tails.
And ooh la la, watch the gallant grooms

strut their stuff, the puffed-up lek males
performing their version of a pole dance,
tucking in their bills, vying for the females,

eyeing up their prospects, their chance
of a future. The future has some hope now,
thanks to Secretary Jewell taking a stance.

The grouse is saved, the end of a protracted row.
The whole sage-swaying sea is singing hallelujah,
along with elk, pronghorn, mule deer, globemallow.

Good news for all sheltered under this umbrella
been blown inside out. Folks spoke up and *voilà!*

Wheat

The old gods are defunct, but not the old necessity
to give thanks. This god spread from the Levant
forgotten religions ago, bestowing prosperity.

He is goodness incarnate, the Midas plant
without the Midas curse, turning a field
into plains of swaying gold. He is our constant

from dawn to dawn, strength concealed
within burnished stalks of energy,
grounded goodness variously revealed.

This great shape-changer: the deity
of cereal, pasta, bread, the English taco
has more lives than Buddha. We

become him, where he grows we grow,
rising each morning, leavened dough.

X

Surely there are others in your life who
make you feel worthwhile, are a safe haven.
I am lucky enough to have a staple few.

And now this other, a befriending dolphin
I swam out deep again to meet. I can't tell
even myself what I felt when I first saw the fin

slice through the surface, the swell,
then to see this undine, stock-still at my feet.
We looked each other in the eyes for well

over a minute, a millennium. His sweet,
kind gaze. I wonder what he made of me
in only my pelt and goggles. What a treat:

to be allowed to touch his grinning head before he
undulated back across Dingle Bay, the channel's Lethe.

Y

is the divining rod, the wishbone, the question
why one y rather than another why:
the yak, the y tree, the yellow-eyed penguin

or the myriad y insects who crawl and fly
we know nothing of, nor will ever know?
The links break from alpha, beyond why.

You mention the Yaqui chub, a minnow,
or Yaqui catfish sporting Chinese whiskers,
both Yaquis depending on the slow flow

of Yaqui River. According to Surem elders
—the last to speak Yaqui, Yoeme Niki, Hiaki
(and where do languages go when they die, others

on the brink?)—the Surem's goddess, Yumululi,
speaks through The Great Tree, divines our future history.

Zanzibar Leopard

Lore about the Zanzibar leopard included the belief that wavyale (witches) sent them to harm villagers, and so they were killed on sight. After the Zanzibar Revolution of 1964, there was a leopard-extermination campaign, which sealed the leopard's extinction.

Kill evil incatinate. Kill kill kill
the Zanzibar leopard, this island devil,
this vampire vermin, obeying witch-will,

dispatched by *wavyale* to bedevil
villages. You know the old strategy:
demonize, and the demonizer will revel

in playing God, the paw of the Almighty.
This leopard survived since the ice age,
slowly shrunk itself into dwarf-cat royalty,

even changed its spots, but couldn't manage
to outwit human categorizing. Yes, it is daft,
but this cat's hardly likely to be found in a cage

or ruling the night forest now. When statecraft
bands with religion, there's no better witchcraft.

Envoy

ZAYANTE

There's something off about talk of the land
as a person, it being more a moody personality
that you insecurely feel, project, understand

via the osmosis of yourself, your ability
to shape change, the abracadabra
matching outside to within. Take Zayante,

home of the slender gilia, Bonny Doon manzanita,
coast horned lizard, band-winged grasshopper,
Ben Lomond spineflower, June beetle, ponderosa,

kangaroo rat, all going beyond a whimper.
People's needs, comforts, fears up the ante.
The development night by day grows grimmer.

Which *ciao* will it be, hi or goodbye, on Planet Zayante?
Enough Gregorian cant and rant. We're done. *Adelante.*

ACKNOWLEDGMENTS
AND NOTES

Grateful acknowledgment is made to the editors of the following publications, in which the poems listed, some under different titles and/or in slightly different versions, first appeared: *Atlantic:* "Breaking News" and "Earthworm"; *Best of Poetry London:* "While Reading the Diary of Christopher Columbus"; *Boston Compass* "*Bos taurus*" and "Golden Toad"; *The Finest Music: An Anthology of Early Irish Lyrics:* "From *The Vision of Mac Conglinne*"; *Literary Imagination:* "Aye-Aye," "Dusky Seaside Sparrow," "Honeybee," and "The Lion"; *New Humanist:* "Photoautotrophs"; *Poetry Ireland Review:* "Monarch Butterfly"; *Poetry Review:* "S"; *Selected Delanty:* "Loosestrife"; *So Little Time: Words and Images for a World in Climate Crisis:* "Apathy Is Out" and "Canticle of the Sun."

For help with the translation "Apathy Is Out" I would like to acknowledge Liam Ó Muirthilé, who also helped me, along with Laney Presto-Matto, with "From *The Vision of Mac Conglinne*."

Any proceeds received by me from this collection will go to 350.org.

I would like to thank John Bourke, David Cavanagh, Cathy Dillon, John FitzGerald, Edna Longley, Michael Longley, Thomas McCarthy, Paul McLoughlin, Michael Palma, Christopher Ricks, Maurice Riordan and Jonathan Williams, who all helped me with this book.

Part 1. "Chimpanzee" is from an account by Jane Goodall.

Part 2. "Pumping Gas": The goal of reaching 350 parts per million of carbon dioxide in the earth's atmosphere is based on what is thought to be the highest level of carbon dioxide in the atmosphere to avoid the worst effects of climate change.

"Earthworm": "From earthworms we learn that before anything grows there has to be prepared soil. When we talk about the endless process of bringing briefs and information to government, the only thing that can keep us going is the notion that it prepares the soil. It may not change minds, but it will provide the arguments for a time when minds are changed. Unless there is that prepared soil, no new thoughts and no new ways of dealing with problems will ever arise." From the obituary of Ursula Franklin, *Globe and Mail,* Canada

Part 3. "Zanzibar Leopard": In 2018, a leopard was possibly recorded on a camera trap, thus renewing hopes for the population's survival.

CPSIA information can be obtained
at www.ICGtesting.com
Printed in the USA
LVHW020045290920
667360LV00003B/897